Gooney d

Gooney Bird Is So Absurd

by
LOIS LOWRY

Illustrated by Middy Thomas

sandpiper

HOUGHTON MIFFLIN HARCOURT
Boston New York

www.hmhbooks.com

The text of this book is set in Garamond MT.

The Library of Congress has cataloged the hardcover edition as follows:
Lowry, Lois.
Gooney Bird is so absurd/by Lois Lowry
p. cm.
Summary: Mrs. Pidgeon's second-grade class studies poetry and her
students write haiku, couplets, free verse, and finally, a tribute to
Mrs. Pidgeon's mother organized by the irrepressible Gooney Bird Greene.
[1. Poetry—Fiction. 2. School—Fiction.] I. Title.
PZ7.L9673Goi 2002

ISBN: 978-0-547-11967-0 hardcover
ISBN: 978-0-547-87559-0 paperback

Manufactured in the United States of America
DOC 10 9 8 7 6 5 4 3 2 1
4500390448

For Emilia Jansson

1.

Mr. Leroy's voice crackled through the intercom speaker after a fifth-grader named Henry Newmeyer had led the entire school in the Pledge of Allegiance.

"This is your principal, Mr. Leroy," he said, and Mrs. Pidgeon's second-graders all laughed. They knew he was their principal. He didn't need to tell them. It wasn't like the day in October when Gooney Bird Greene had appeared in their classroom for the first time and said, "I'm your new student." She'd *needed* to explain that, because nobody had had a clue who she was, and she had arrived wearing pajamas and cowboy boots, which made her somewhat mysterious.

But everyone already knew who Mr. Leroy was. He was Watertower Elementary's principal and he was the best principal, the children thought, in the whole world. He was smart and funny and he wore the most interesting neckties, except for the blue striped one. He had explained that his wife's mother had given him the blue striped one for his birthday, so he felt that he had to wear it now and then. He really thought it was a boring necktie, but if they ever met his mother-in-law they should not tell her that he thought that.

"I just want to alert you all to the weather forecast," Mr. Leroy's voice continued through the intercom. "I guess we shouldn't be surprised, since it is January, but the prediction is for snow tomorrow.

"Walkers? Be sure to wear warm boots and mittens," he said.

"That's me," Ben announced from his desk. "I'm a walker! I'm wearing my L.L.Bean boots tomorrow!"

"Me, too," Nicholas chimed in. "I'm a walker, too."

"And bus people?" Mr. Leroy went on.

"Me," Keiko said in her very quiet voice.

"And me," Chelsea announced. "I get on Bus Eleven at the corner of Cherry Street."

"Be sure to be extra well behaved on the bus," Mr. Leroy reminded them, "because the driving might be difficult in the snow. We want all of our drivers to pay careful attention to the slippery roads, not to children who might be noisy or wiggly."

"That's you, Malcolm!" someone called out. Malcolm grinned. It was true; he did have trouble sitting still. He was wiggling back and forth in his seat at this very moment.

"Of course," Mr. Leroy continued, "if there is a *lot* of snow, you know what that means!"

"Snow day!" the children all called out.

"Snow day! OKAY!" Tyrone shouted.

"Snow day," Mr. Leroy said, like an echo, even though he couldn't hear Mrs. Pidgeon's classroom from his office. "But let's hope not. We all have lots of schoolwork to get done, don't we?

"Now," he added, "some of you have noticed that I'm wearing my reptile tie this morning."

Mrs. Pidgeon laughed. "Yes, he is," she said. "I saw it when I was having coffee in the teachers' lounge. It gives me the creeps."

"I love that one," Beanie said. "It has iguanas and everything!"

"Komodo dragons!" Barry added.

"Oh, gross," murmured Keiko, who hated anything that might possibly be slimy.

"Shhh," Mrs. Pidgeon said, still laughing. She pointed to the speaker and reminded them to keep listening to the principal's voice.

"So I'll sign off by saying: 'See you later—'"

"Alligator!" the second-graders called out as the intercom went silent. Throughout the school, each class said "Alligator!" and then Watertower Elementary School fell silent as the teachers and children began their day.

☆ ☆ ☆

"Well, class," Mrs. Pidgeon said, "as you all know, usually I begin each morning by—"

"Mrs. Pidgeon! Mrs. Pidgeon!" Barry Tuckerman was halfway out of his seat, waving his hand in the air.

Mrs. Pidgeon sighed. "What is it, Barry?" she asked.

"Look at what Gooney Bird's *wearing*!" Barry said loudly, and pointed toward the desk where Gooney Bird Greene had just opened her spelling book.

All of the children giggled. They frequently giggled at Gooney Bird's outfits. Ever since her first day as a new student, when she had worn pajamas to school, they had been amazed and astonished and amused and awed at the things she decided to wear. A ballet tutu, sometimes. Dangly rhinestone earrings once, though she took them off when her earlobes began to ache. Hiking boots with an organdy pinafore. Sandals with unmatched knee socks.

Today Gooney Bird was wearing an over-size tie-dyed sweatshirt. She had worn that particular shirt to school before, so it wasn't unusual. But today she had something on her head. A sort of a pale green helmet with ruffles and two holes through which her red ponytails poked out.

Gooney Bird looked up when she heard the giggles. "What?" she said. "I'm trying to study for the spelling test. I can never remember whether it's an *a* or an *e* in *separate*."

"We were just noticing your, ah, your head-piece," Mrs. Pidgeon commented.

"Yes. It's my two-ponytail hat. On days

when I have just *one* ponytail, I wear a baseball cap with my one ponytail sticking through the hole in back. But this morning I was brushing my teeth when I looked in the bathroom mirror and I said to myself, 'Gooney Bird, I do believe today is a two-ponytail day!'"

"I've seen you with your baseball cap on, Gooney Bird," Mrs. Pidgeon said, "but never with this, ah, two-ponytail hat before."

"It's brand new." Gooney Bird turned her head to give the teacher a side view of the pale green ruffles and the ponytail holes. "Do you like it?"

"Well, it's unusual," Mrs. Pidgeon replied. "I'll say that for it."

"It's *underpants!*" Chelsea shrieked. The entire class roared with laughter.

Gooney Bird sighed. She waited patiently until the class became quiet again. Then she said, "Chelsea, Chelsea, Chelsea. Whatever am I going to do with you? You *know* what that word does to the class! Remember when we were writing stories and I explained that you could always get a laugh with *armpit* or *belly-button* or *underpants*? But that's a cheap laugh."

She looked back at her spelling book. "It's an *a*. I have to remember that. *Desperate* has an *e* but *separate* has an *a*. It's very confusing."

"My mom and dad are separated," Tricia said with a sigh, "and it's very confusing because I live in two houses, and sometimes my crayons are in one house but my coloring book is in the other."

"My mom and dad are *desperate*," Malcolm said, "because they had triplets."

The class laughed. They all knew about the commotion the triplet babies were causing in Malcolm's family.

"I see London, I see France," Ben called in a singsong voice. "I see Gooney's—"

"Enough," announced Mrs. Pidgeon. She glanced suddenly at Tyrone. "Tyrone, what do I see in your hand?"

Tyrone put on his who-me-I'm-very-inno-cent face. Mrs. Pidgeon went to his desk and reached out her hand. "You know the rules, Tyrone," she said, and he handed her the small cell phone.

"It's for emergencies," he said defensively.

"And what sort of emergency do you antic-ipate?"

"Ah, a bear may be comin' into the class-room."

"A *bear*," murmured all the other second-graders.

"In come a bear, but Tyrone doan care, when the kids all yell he just dial his cell . . ."

Mrs. Pidgeon, who usually enjoyed Tyrone's raps, glared at him and dropped the cell phone into the top drawer of her desk. "As I was about to say, I usually begin each morning reading a poem."

"Oh, I love when you do that. I love po-emth," Felicia Ann said. Her top front teeth were slow in coming in and she had a gap there that made it hard for her to say an *s*.

"That was a poem I was saying," Ben pointed out. "*France* rhymes with—"

Mrs. Pidgeon strode to his desk and clamped a hand on his shoulder. "And this morning," she continued, still with her restraining hand on Ben but smiling at Felicia Ann, "I had chosen a winter poem to read, but then suddenly, when Mr. Leroy was talking over the intercom about a snowstorm on the way, Tyrone, you . . ." She looked over at Tyrone, who was busy folding a piece of paper into a cootie-catcher.

He glanced up at the sound of his name. "Who, me? I didn't do nuthin!" Then he corrected himself. "*Anything,* I meant. I didn't do anything."

Mrs. Pidgeon laughed. "It wasn't anything you did. It was what you said. You said . . ." She looked around at the children. "Anyone remember? Tyrone said, 'Snow day . . .'"

"'Okay!'" several children called. "'Snow day! Okay!' That's what he said!"

Mrs. Pidgeon nodded. "And it occurred to me that Tyrone had created our morning poem with just those three words."

The class fell silent. They looked at her. Beanie raised her hand. When the teacher nodded at her, she said with a frown, "It can't be a poem. It's too short."

"There are no rules about how long a poem should be," Mrs. Pidgeon said. "It only has to be long enough to say what you want it to say. And here is what Tyrone wanted to say." She went to the board. Carefully, in her neat printing, she wrote:

SNOW DAY!
OKAY!

The class looked at the words. Malcolm, who could never remember to raise his hand, called, "No way!"

With the eraser, Mrs. Pidgeon removed the words. She smiled. Then she wrote:

SNOW DAY!
NO WAY!

Malcolm read it and grinned. "I made a poem!" he said in a surprised, proud voice.

"I did mine already," Tyrone pointed out. "Snow day! Okay!"

"Me, too," said Malcolm. "Snow day! No way!"

"I have one!" Keiko said, raising her hand. "Can I write mine on the board?" Mrs. Pidgeon gave her the chalk and Keiko wrote:

SNOW DAY!
LET'S PLAY!

Next Tricia wrote:

SNOW DAY!
HOORAY!

"I never knew a poem could be little," Felicia Ann said in her soft, shy voice.

"A poem can be whatever you make it be," Gooney Bird pointed out. She got up from her desk, took her turn at the board, and wrote:

SNOW DAY!
I'LL SAY!

Mrs. Pidgeon looked at Gooney Bird as she stood at the board with her two red ponytails protruding from the ruffled holes. "I'm sorry, but I have to ask this," she said. "I don't mean to get a cheap laugh. But, Gooney Bird, *are* those underpants on your head?"

Gooney Bird thought for a moment. Then she said, in a patient voice, "*Once* it was underpants. Now it's a two-ponytail hat. It's like a poem. It can be whatever you want it to be.

"Actually," she went on, and reached for the ruffled fabric, "I'm going to take it off now. The elastic hurts my forehead."

"Gooney Bird," said Mrs. Pidgeon with a smile, "you're so absurd!"

Gooney Bird grinned. "Aha! A poem!" she pointed out.

"Look!" she said suddenly, turning toward the window. Outside, they could see the first flakes of snow beginning to fall.

2.

By the next morning there was snow everywhere, but not enough to cancel school. The buses arrived one by one, their wheels slurping through the slush and shooting wet snow along the edge of the sidewalk so that the walkers, the children who lived near the school, had to jump aside.

Gooney Bird Greene entered the classroom with the other children, and they began to remove hats and mittens and jackets and boots. They all kept indoor footwear in their cubbies. One by one they lined up their wet boots and changed into their dry slippers and clogs and Crocs.

"What on earth are those, Gooney Bird?" Mrs. Pidgeon asked, watching as Gooney Bird sat on the floor and tried to wrestle something off her feet.

Gooney Bird scowled. "Well," she said, "I *thought* they were high-fashion boots. I got them at the Goodwill store, on the half-price table. One dollar and forty-five cents."

"Quite a bargain," Mrs. Pidgeon commented, still looking at Gooney Bird's feet. "Need some help?"

"Thank you." Gooney Bird hobbled to a nearby bench, sat down, and held her legs out. One at a time Mrs. Pidgeon pulled off the wet boots. They were bright blue, with very high, thin heels.

When Mrs. Pidgeon had set them side by side on the shelf, next to the long puddled row of ordinary rubber boots, Gooney Bird looked

at them with distaste. "I thought the stiletto heels were very cool," she said. "*Stiletto* means a thin, pointy stabbing tool, and that's why they call these stiletto heels. See?" She held one up. "But they're not comfortable. They *do* stab. And they were slippery on the ice. I fell twice on my way to school. Look. My knees are all wet."

Mrs. Pidgeon felt the damp knees of Gooney Bird's black tights sympathetically. "Goodness," she said.

"I have buyer's remorse," Gooney Bird said.

"What'th that?" asked Felicia Ann, who was nearby, watching.

"It's when you wish you hadn't bought something," Gooney Bird explained. "I hardly ever have it. I make my purchases carefully. But today I have a bad case of buyer's remorse about those dumb boots." She looked at them with a frown and slid her feet into the soft bunny slippers she kept in her cubby.

"My dad has buyer's remorse about our car," Ben said. "It always needs repairs, and it's noisy." He drove an imaginary car across his desk and made a roaring sound.

"My mom has buyer's remorse about a bottle of milk she bought at the corner store!" Malcolm said. "It was too old and when she opened it she made a face at the smell. It smelled like barf!"

Mrs. Pidgeon held up her hand to ask for quiet, because it was clear that all of the second-graders were going to start making barfing noises. She went to the front of the room and picked up a folder from her desk. She took a paper out of the folder and looked at it with a smile.

"Today's poem," she announced. "See if you can guess why I chose it."

She began to read but was interrupted after the first two words. "'Over the—'"

"Please excuse me for interrupting, Mrs.

Pidgeon," Keiko said, with her hand up. "But you must always, always start by saying the title and the author's name. You taught us that."

"Tyrone used to say 'Arthur' instead of 'author,'" Malcolm, chortling, reminded everyone. "Remember? Remember when Tyrone thought it was 'Arthur'? All poems were written by Arthur? Is Tyrone dumb or *what?*"

Mrs. Pidgeon, still holding the paper, went to Malcolm's desk and put her calm-down hand on his shoulder.

"Actually, there are probably many poets named Arthur, so it may be that Tyrone was smarter about poetry than most of us. And we all certainly know what a good poet Tyrone is, when he creates his raps! Got one now, Tyrone?"

Tyrone, whose face had turned very glum, brightened up. He snapped his fingers and thought for a minute. *"Soon as I git home, gonna write me a pome—"* he chanted.

"Good. Maybe we *all* will. Maybe that could be our homework tonight," Mrs. Pidgeon said. "And you're right, Keiko. It *is* correct to read the title and the author's name—which in many cases could, in fact, be Arthur"—she glanced at Malcolm—"but for the moment I'm simply going to read the poem, and then I'll explain the title and tell you the author. Okay. Ready? Shall I begin again?"

All of the children nodded.

In a quiet, clear voice, Mrs. Pidgeon read:

> Over the pavement
> Snow falls in January—
> Soap flakes wash our tracks

"It'th another *little* poem," Felicia Ann pointed out.

"It doesn't rhyme," Barry Tuckerman said. "All of our snow day poems rhymed."

"It's nice, though," Tricia said. "It makes a picture in my head."

"Poems don't *have* to rhyme," Beanie reminded them.

"I see London, I see France . . . *That*
rhymes," Ben called out. "*France* rhymes
with—" He stopped, aware that Mrs. Pidgeon
was glaring at him. "Sorry," he said. "Cheap
laugh."

"Oh, Mrs. Pidgeon, Mrs. Pidgeon!" Keiko
churned her arm in the air. It was unlike quiet
Keiko to be so excited. Her face was pink with
enthusiasm.

"What is it, Keiko?"

Keiko stood beside her desk. "It's haiku,
isn't it?" she said, grinning. "It's haiku! I recog-
nize it! *Haiku* is Japanese!"

Keiko's family was Japanese American. Her
grandparents had grown up in Japan, though
they lived now with her whole family in the
town of Watertower. She had gone back with
them once, to Yokohama, for a visit. She had
sent a postcard with a picture of Mount Fuji to

Mrs. Pidgeon; the postcard was still on the bulletin board.

"That's correct. And in fact," Mrs. Pidgeon said, "that's the reason I didn't start with the title. The title of this poem is simply 'Haiku.'"

"Is it by an Arthur?" asked Nicholas.

She laughed. "No," she said.

"It's by a Japanese person, stupid!" called Malcolm.

"I bet Daisuke wrote it, right?" said Ben. "He's Japanese."

Mrs. Pidgeon wrinkled her forehead. "Who is Daisuke?" she asked.

All of the boys began to laugh. Mrs. Pidgeon was not a sports fan, and Daisuke was a famous baseball player. Nicholas explained that to her.

"Oh," she said. "Thank you. I didn't know that. And maybe Daisuke *does* write poems while he's sitting in the—what is that place called? The *birchbark*?"

"The *dugout!*" the boys all yelled.

Mrs. Pidgeon laughed. "I knew that. I was just teasing. But no, this haiku isn't by Daisuke. In fact, it isn't by a Japanese person. The Japanese invented haiku, that's true; but anyone is allowed to use the form. And the author of this haiku is actually our room mother."

The children were silent for a moment. "But our room mother is *your* mother!" Chelsea said at last.

"That's true."

"She's Mrs. X!" said Beanie.

Mrs. Pidgeon laughed. "Well, that's what we all called her for a while when she was being mysterious and didn't want us to guess who she was."

"I remember when she came from the nursing home and brought us cupcakes," Tricia said. "She's very, very old."

"That's true," Mrs. Pidgeon said. "My mother is very, very old. And she's not very well at the moment, so I've been spending a lot of time at the nursing home with her. I opened up an old trunk filled with things from her past, and I found all these poems that she had written. I sit by her bed and read them to her. She likes that. Yesterday, when I read this haiku, I decided it would be a good one for our morning poem."

"Mrs. Pidgeon! I have a poem! I just made it up!" Malcolm called.

The teacher sighed. "All right, Malcolm," she said.

Malcolm stood. He said in a loud voice:

> HAIKU!
> KUNG FU!

He made his hands into fists, struck a pose, and kicked one leg into the air.

When all of the boys began to arrange themselves in martial-arts poses, Mrs. Pidgeon quickly went to the piano and played a few soft chords. It was her best method for calming down the entire class. It always worked.

When they were quiet and calm, she said, "I'm just going to describe the rules of haiku to you quickly, and then we must go on to our math."

She wrote her mother's poem on the board:

> Over the pavement
> Snow falls in January—
> Soap flakes wash our tracks

They all read it aloud together.

"Okay," said Mrs. Pidgeon. "Three lines. Five syllables in the first line."

They read the first line slowly so that they could hear the syllables. Five.

"Next line: seven," said Mrs. Pidgeon.

They read the second line and could hear that it was true. Seven syllables.

"Finally, five again, in the third line," she told them, and they read it aloud.

"Usually, a haiku is about one of the seasons," she explained. "This one, of course, is about winter. It describes snow, in January. What other seasons do we have?"

"Thummer!" said Felicia Ann. "Thpring!"

"Correct. And fall, or autumn. So there we have the basic rules of haiku. Later today we'll have time to give writing haiku a try. But right now"—she looked at the clock—"we really must get to our math problems."

Then Mrs. Pidgeon noticed that Gooney Bird Greene, who had been very quiet, had her hand raised. "Yes, Gooney Bird?"

"I wrote one," Gooney Bird said. "I know I should have been facing forward, hands folded, eyes on you, when you were talking. But I couldn't help myself. Sometimes you just can't help yourself." She held up a lined paper with some writing on it.

"I know. That's true sometimes. All right, Gooney Bird, why don't you read it to the class? Then: math."

Gooney Bird stood. Frowning, she adjusted the damp knees of her tights. Then she read, from her paper:

Haiku
by Gooney Bird Greene

Winter walk to school
Stiletto boots, icy street—
Toes and knees suffer

3.

After the next morning's intercom announcements were over, Mrs. Pidgeon went to the front of the class with a paper in her hand.

"Is your mother better?" Beanie asked.

Mrs. Pidgeon looked sad. "No," she said, "I'm afraid not. When you're very old, as my mother is, you just start to give out, and you don't get better. But yesterday after school, I went to see her and I read poems to her again. Her own poems. You know, at one time my mom was a very serious writer."

"Is that one of hers?" Barry asked, pointing to the paper. Mrs. Pidgeon nodded.

"Another haiku?" asked Keiko.

"No, this one is different. I know some of you like hearing poems that rhyme, so I looked through my mother's poetry and found a lovely rhyming one."

"I hope it's not *long*," said Malcolm. "That poem you read at Halloween was *long*."

Mrs. Pidgeon laughed. "Anybody remember the name of that one?" she asked the second-graders. "Barry? You're my student who remembers *everything*. You're the memory champion of the class."

Barry grinned and nodded. "It was 'Little Orphan Annie,' and the name of the author was James Whitcomb Reilly."

"Good for you! That's correct. I read that one because it was about goblins and scary things, so it seemed just right for Halloween. But you're right, Malcolm—it was quite long."

Gooney Bird raised her hand. It made a clanking sound because she was wearing a large number of bracelets on that arm. Gooney Bird liked jewelry a lot.

"Sorry for the clank," she said. "I'm taking my bracelets off in a minute because they make it hard for me to write. They clank on the desk."

"How about the gloves?" asked Mrs. Pidgeon. "They don't interfere with your writing?" Gooney Bird was also wearing her fingerless gloves.

"Nope. Actually, I think they help with writing, because they keep my writing hand warm and make words flow out onto the paper better. It's like when I warm my brain with a hat."

"I see. Did you have a question? Is that why you raised your hand?"

"No, I just wanted to say something about long-ness. I think a poem should be just smack exactly as long as it tells you it should be."

"As it tells you?" Mrs. Pidgeon repeated, with a puzzled look.

Gooney Bird nodded. She pulled her bracelets off and stacked them on her desktop, carefully making a round tower of the brass circles. "Yes. Writing a poem is the same as writing a story. You say what you want to say, and then it tells you, in your brain: *Stop here.*"

"Hmmm," said the teacher, thinking. "I believe you're right, and that we should all listen more carefully to our brains."

"You might try warming your brains with a hat," Gooney Bird suggested politely.

Malcolm held up his fist and pretended it was a microphone. "Brain to Malcolm, Brain to Malcolm," he intoned in a deep voice. "'Wear underpants on your head.'"

"Teacher to Malcolm," Mrs. Pidgeon said, holding up her own invisible microphone. "I am going to read this morning's poem now, and I want you to pay attention. You were one of the ones who wanted rhyme."

Standing in front of the class, Mrs. Pidgeon carefully unfolded the paper and read aloud:

My Daughter
by Mrs. X

"Hey!" Tyrone called out. "That's you! If your mom write that, then you be the daughter, right?"

"That's true," said Mrs. Pidgeon. "This is a poem about me. My mother wrote it many years ago, so it's a poem about me when I was your age."

"Cool," said Tyrone.

"Mrs. Pidgeon, you ought to say the author's real name, not 'Mrs. X'! Just because we call her Mrs. X, that doesn't mean it's her author name!" Chelsea pointed out.

"You're correct, Chelsea. But you know what, class? My mother has something special about her name, and I want to surprise you with it. But not yet. So for now, her author name is going to be Mrs. X. Is that all right?"

All of the children nodded.

"I'll start again."

My Daughter
by Mrs. X

Daughter, laughter: spelled the same.
Patricia: my laughing daughter's name.

Mrs. Pidgeon picked up the chalk and wrote the two words on the board: *daughter, laughter.*

"Yep, they oughta rhyme," Tyrone said. "Look at that. It's crazy that they don't rhyme."

"That poem wasn't long," Malcolm said in a relieved voice.

"It's very thweet," Felicia Ann said.

"But it tells a lie!" Nicholas announced. "You said your mom wrote it. So her daughter's name ought to be . . ." He hesitated, thinking.

Mrs. Pidgeon smiled. "That's my first name, Patricia. Some people call me Patsy, or Pat. But my mother always liked my full name best: Patricia."

She read the short poem to them again. "It's just two lines," she pointed out. "Two rhyming lines. Hear that? *Same,* and *name*?"

The children nodded. They said the words aloud: *Same. Name.*

"This kind of poem is called a couplet. Two lines, rhyming. Probably pretty easy to write, I'm guessing. So here's the assignment, class. During our writing time today, I want each of you to try writing a couplet. Then, at the end of the day, we'll read our couplets aloud."

"Do they have to be about Patricias?" Malcolm asked with a scowl.

"No, no. But that's a good question, Malcolm. And I have an idea. Let's do this. Let's each write a couplet about our *own* family. Okay?"

Malcolm sighed. He lived in a very noisy, complicated family because of the triplets that had been born the previous spring. Malcolm was still adjusting to that. "Here's a poem about *my* family," he said with another scowl. "*Crash. Bash. Smash.* That's what it sounds like at my house most of the time."

"Wait till writing time after lunch, Malcolm,"

Mrs. Pidgeon suggested, "and maybe you'll be able to come up with a couplet about triplets. Goodness!" She laughed. "Couplet, triplets? That's almost a rhyme, isn't it?"

Malcolm just rolled his eyes.

✧ ✧ ✧

Writing time took longer than usual. The children, most of them, found that writing poems was not easy. They had to search their heads for the perfect words.

"In stories or fables, you can use *any* old words," Chelsea said, looking glumly at her paper, which was covered with scribbles and cross-outs. "But for a poem, the words have to be *just right*. It's hard."

"Revise, revise, revise," murmured Tricia, her head bent over her desk.

Mrs. Pidgeon moved around the room, talking with those who were having trouble, making suggestions, giving help.

"I don't need help," Barry Tuckerman boasted. "Mine's done. I'm probably the best poet in the world." He turned his paper over and sat with his hands folded.

"You're a poet and you don't know it, but your feet show it—" Ben chanted, looking at Barry. The other children all joined in: *"They're Longfellows!"*

Mrs. Pidgeon looked at the clock. "All right," she said. "I know many of you need more time, but you'll have to stop for now and maybe finish at home because the bell will ring before we know it. Who's ready to read a couplet aloud? Barry, I know you are. Want to start?"

Barry Tuckerman went to the front of the room. The children all giggled. They liked Barry. He was smart and interesting. But he was like an old man: serious and scholarly. And now he stood holding his paper, shoulders back, looking around, waiting for the audience to be attentive.

He cleared his throat. Then he read his poem:

A Couplet
by Barry Tuckerman, author

Sibling is the word for sister or brother.
I don't believe there's any other.

He bowed. The second-graders all clapped. Malcolm gave a shrill whistle of approval.

"That was terrific, Barry," Mrs. Pidgeon told him. "It was—well, it was *Barry-esque.*"

"Does Barry get an A?" asked Chelsea.

"No grade for poetry," Mrs. Pidgeon said. "Poetry is not something you judge. You just savor it."

When she realized they looked puzzled, she suggested, "You can look *savor* up in your dictionaries later." Then she looked around the room. "Anyone else? Good. Felicia Ann is ready."

Felicia Ann went to the front of the room with her paper. Everyone smiled. At one time, Felicia Ann had been so shy that she had always looked at the floor and rarely spoke. But that was changing. Even though her missing teeth were still giving her speech problems, Felicia Ann had begun to be an enthusiastic, sometimes even talkative member of the class.

From the front of the room, she asked the teacher a question. "Doeth it have to have 'Couplet' ath a title? Becauth I have a different title."

"Oh my, no," Mrs. Pidgeon told her. "You are the complete ruler of the title. Whatever you want it to be."

"Good," Felicia Ann replied. "My title ith 'Neethe.'"

"Neethe?" asked Beanie. "What's that?"

"Let's wait and see," Mrs. Pidgeon suggested. "Go ahead, Felicia Ann."

Felicia Ann took a deep breath. Her face

was pink with excitement. She looked at her paper and read:

Neethe
by Felithia Ann

Thuthan ith my little neethe.
She doethn't yet have any teeth.

Everyone was silent for a moment as if translating a foreign language. Then they got it, one by one.

"Her niece!"

"Remember Felicia Ann's big sister had a baby?"

"It's Susan! That's her niece's name!"

"Right!" said Felicia Ann. "Thuthan!" She beamed with pride while the class applauded her couplet. Then she sat down.

"Time for maybe two more," Mrs. Pidgeon said. She looked around. "Malcolm. Your turn."

Malcolm bounded to the front of the room. His shoes were untied, his shirt buttons were in the wrong holes, and there were Magic Marker stains all over his hands.

His paper was crumpled, but he smoothed it out and read in a loud voice:

Triplets
by Malcolm

Some people have siblings and some not any.
I have three. That's two too many.

The class laughed and clapped, and Malcolm folded his paper into an airplane and sailed it across the room. It missed the hamster cage and rested on a stack of *National Geographic*s.

"Sometimes poetry is a good way of explaining our feelings, isn't it?" Mrs. Pidgeon said. "Thank you, Malcolm. Good work. Now: who's next? Last one today!"

"I'll go," Gooney Bird announced. She

stood. Today, in addition to her brain-warming hat and her fingerless gloves, the ones that she said warmed and invigorated her writing hands, she was also wearing a fur collar at the neck of her sweatshirt. The left leg of her jeans was rolled up to her knee so that her striped knee sock showed above her bunny slipper.

"My poem tells my feelings, too," she said, "and it's a shortie, so I memorized it and I don't need to read it from the paper. But . . ." Gooney Bird looked around. "Could some of you come up and stand here with me while I say it?"

"Why?" asked Chelsea. "Are you scared?"

"I am *never* scared," Gooney Bird replied.

"Embarrathed?" asked Felicia Ann.

"I am *never* embarrassed," Gooney Bird said.

"Why do you need us, then?" asked Keiko.

"Because you are part of my poem. Sometimes a poem is more than just words."

"Well, *I'll* be a part of Gooney Bird's poem," Mrs. Pidgeon announced. "It would be an honor." She went and stood beside Gooney Bird at the front of the room.

"Me, too!" said Beanie.

"And me!"

"I want to, too!"

One by one the children got up from their desks and went to stand in increasingly long lines on both sides of Gooney Bird Greene. The lines made their way around the border of the room, past the hamster cage, past the art display, past the large calendar on the wall.

"We're a thircle!" Felicia Ann pointed out.

"Now," Gooney Bird instructed, "hold hands, everyone!"

She removed her fingerless gloves and took the hand of Mrs. Pidgeon on one side and Malcolm on the other. Around the circle every child reached out and held hands on both sides.

Gooney Bird looked around. "Okay," she

said, when they were all arranged. "Here's my poem." In a firm, clear voice, she recited:

Child
by Gooney Bird Greene

I'm an only.
But not lonely.

4.

"You promised funny today, Mrs. Pidgeon! You said we could do funny poems!" Ben said.

"I did indeed," Mrs. Pidgeon told the class. "Humorous poems today." She went to the board and wrote a word: LIMERICK.

Just then there was a knock on the classroom door. It opened, and Mr. Leroy, the principal, came in. Today he was wearing his chess-game tie, with little knights and pawns and other chess pieces on it in a pattern. "Just visiting," he said with a smile. "Got room for me?"

Mrs. Pidgeon, still standing at the board,

pulled her chair away from her desk and gestured to Mr. Leroy. "Oh good," he said as he sat down in the teacher's chair. "Thank you. I don't mind sitting at a child's desk, but my knees are always stiff afterward."

"Class, shall we tell Mr. Leroy what we're studying?"

"Poetry!" the second-graders said loudly, all together.

Mr. Leroy made a face. "I was hoping you'd be studying volcanoes. I'm afraid poetry might be *booorring*."

The children were silent for a moment. So was Mrs. Pidgeon. Then Gooney Bird stood at her seat. Today she was wearing a fringed cowboy vest over her denim overalls. Gooney Bird put her hands on her hips. "Mr. Leroy," she said, "I am *shocked* that you would say that!"

"Yeth!" Felicia Ann said. "Me, too!"

"So," Mr. Leroy said, "poetry isn't boring?"

"No!" the entire class said.

"It's hard, though," Tyrone pointed out. "You gotta work hard to get it right. Every word gotta be right."

"You have to learn about couplets and stuff," Ben said.

"And haiku," Keiko added.

"And today," Mrs. Pidgeon told the principal, "we are going to do . . ." She pointed to the word she had written on the board. "Limericks."

"Funny poems!" Malcolm called out.

Mr. Leroy leaned back in the chair. "Well," he said. "I think I'll stay for a while! I'd like to learn about funny poems myself!"

"Did your mother write a limerick, Mrs. Pidgeon?" Gooney Bird asked.

"She did. I'll read her limerick right now, and then I'll describe how we can create our own." The teacher unfolded a paper.

"Mrs. Pidgeon's mom was a poet," Tricia whispered to Mr. Leroy in explanation.

"Is," Gooney Bird corrected. "Once you're a poet, you're always, always a poet."

"And your feet show it, 'cuz they're Long-fellows," Malcolm added. "Sorry," he said, when he realized that Mrs. Pidgeon was giving him a look.

"This poem has no title," Mrs. Pidgeon said when the class was quiet and waiting. "It's surprising, but often limericks don't have titles. So I'll just start." She began to read.

> A very rich lady named Dot
> Spent a fortune on buying a yacht,
>> Then let out a wail
>> While trying to sail,
> For it started to float but did not.

The children laughed. "My cousin tipped over in a canoe once!" Barry said.

"I saw *Titanic*! The whole ship sank!" Nicholas said.

"Me, too!"

"I saw *Titanic* too!"

Mrs. Pidgeon played a chord on the piano and the class became quiet. "Boring?" she asked. She was looking at Mr. Leroy.

"Nope. Not boring," Mr. Leroy said with a smile.

"Okay, class. That was a limerick. A limerick is often funny, and it usually begins with a description of a person in the first line. Shall we try creating a limerick together?"

"Yes!" the children called out.

"All right. I'm going to start by giving you a first line. And I'll use my own name."

"No fair!" said Chelsea. "Nothing rhymes with Pidgeon!"

Mrs. Pidgeon chuckled. "It's not necessary to use a last name. How about this?" she suggested. "'There once was a teacher named Pat'?"

She looked around. "Think about words that rhyme with *Pat*. Who can come up with the next line? Hands, please. Don't call out."

For a moment, no hands went up. Everyone sat silently, thinking. Someone murmured, "Fat." Another child said, "Cat," in a low voice. Then, all at once, six hands were raised. Mrs. Pidgeon looked around the room. "Mr. Leroy?" she said, pointing to him. The principal had raised his hand. "Second line?"

"'Who gave up the chair where she sat,'" Mr. Leroy said.

"Cool!" Tyrone called out. "Good job, dude!"

"All right," Mrs. Pidgeon said. "Thank you, Mr. Leroy. Now we have the first two lines." She wrote them on the board. "Next we need two shorter, rhyming lines. Any thoughts, class?"

Again the children and the principal became silent. Suddenly Gooney Bird stood up and said loudly, "Eureka!"

"Eureka?" asked Mrs. Pidgeon.

"That means 'I got it!' You say it when a

great idea comes to you unexpectedly," Gooney Bird explained.

"And a great idea has?"

"Yep!" said Gooney Bird with a grin. "I thought of the whole rest of the limerick. It's a eureka moment."

"Good for you. Would you like to come to the front of the class to recite it?"

"Yes. But wait." Gooney Bird opened the lid of her desk and rummaged inside. She took out something that looked familiar: pale green and ruffled. Today Gooney Bird's hair was not in ponytails. But she grabbed half of her red hair in one hand and pulled it through one leg hole, and then she did the same with the other half. Finally she carefully arranged the elastic waistband around her head and across her forehead. Wearing her headpiece, she went to the front of the room and recited the limerick:

> There once was a teacher named Pat
> Who gave up the chair where she sat.

She tried to write verse,
But it only got worse
Till she warmed up her brain with a hat.

The class applauded. "You may borrow my hat, Mrs. Pidgeon," Gooney Bird said, "anytime you want. Or you can make your own, of course."

"Of course," Mrs. Pidgeon said. "Next? How about each of you try using your own name in a first line? No need to write an entire limerick. Let's start with first lines. I'll walk around the class in case anyone needs help." She looked at the principal. Usually his visits to classrooms lasted only a few minutes. But Mr. Leroy had picked up a paper and pencil and it did not look as if he were planning to leave.

For a few moments the classroom was quiet, with heads bent over, pencils moving on papers. Then, here and there, groaning started.

"Nothing rhymes with my name!" Malcolm groaned. "Nothing!"

Gooney Bird leaned over from her desk and whispered a suggestion. "'A boy who had triplets at home,'" she suggested. "That's a good first line, and it tells about you. It doesn't have to use your name," she said.

"How about *me?*" Keiko wailed.

Mrs. Pidgeon was headed to Keiko's desk when Gooney Bird spoke again. "I have an idea for Keiko, Mrs. Pidgeon! How about 'A young girl of Asian descent'? Lots of things rhyme with *descent*!"

One by one, the children created their first lines. Mrs. Pidgeon wrote every one neatly on the board. Then the class added second, rhyming lines. Some were quite easy; others were very, very hard.

> A boy who had triplets at home
> Sometimes needed a brush and a comb
>
> A young girl of Asian descent
> Decided to live in a tent

A redhead named Gooney Bird Greene
Wore a hat that was hardly routine

There once was a dude named Tyrone
Who frequently talked on the phone

A young girl named Chelsea explained
That she liked to be out when it rained

"Mr. Leroy?" Gooney Bird said when she noticed that the principal was still working. His tongue was wedged between his teeth. "Time to put your pencil down."

"I'm not done," Mr. Leroy said.

Gooney Bird looked at Mrs. Pidgeon and raised her eyebrows as if she were asking a silent question. Mrs. Pidgeon shrugged. "Let's let him continue on his own," she whispered.

Together the class worked on the limericks they had begun while Mr. Leroy, his head bent over his paper, wrote and erased, wrote and erased. Sometimes he sighed and stared out the window.

"He's thinking," Keiko pointed out.

"Yes," said Gooney Bird. "Occasionally it helps to look at the sky and make your mind go blank for a minute. Why don't we all try it, because we're sort of stuck on Tyrone's limerick."

The entire class, including Mrs. Pidgeon (but not Mr. Leroy—he was bent over his paper again), stared through the window at the sky.

"My mind never goes blank!" Malcolm groaned. "My thoughts just keep whirling and whirling!"

"Shhhh," said Gooney Bird. "Silence helps."

Gradually, with breaks for staring at the sky, the class began to finish the limericks on the board. Some were very funny and made them laugh aloud. Mr. Leroy never looked up.

"Okay, class," Mrs. Pidgeon said at last. "We

haven't finished them all, but we did some good ones, and you got to see how limericks work. I'll write these down and read them to my mother this evening."

"They'll make her laugh," Tyrone said. "Especially mine!"

"Yes, they will." Mrs. Pidgeon looked at the board and chuckled. She read Tyrone's limerick aloud.

There once was a dude named Tyrone
Who frequently talked on the phone.
      While having some fun,
      He dialed 911,
And they handcuffed him till he was grown.

"Mine, too!" said Gooney Bird. "Read mine to your mom!"

Mrs. Pidgeon, still laughing, read Gooney Bird's limerick.

A redhead named Gooney Bird Greene
Wore a hat that was hardly routine.

We couldn't complain,
For it warmed up her brain,
And at least it was perfectly clean.

"Oh, my goodness!" Mrs. Pidgeon looked at the clock. "You know what? It's lunchtime already. We spent half the morning on limericks! And we never got to our social studies lesson. I wonder if the principal will be mad at us."

She was looking toward Mr. Leroy when she said that. He didn't hear her. He was looking at his paper and chewing on the eraser at the end of his pencil.

"I bet the principal is gonna *punish* us!" Tyrone said loudly. But Mr. Leroy didn't hear him. He was writing again.

"Earth to Principal!" Malcolm said into his fake microphone. But Mr. Leroy didn't look up.

"Class, on the count of three," Mrs. Pidgeon suggested, "outdoor voices. One . . . two . . . *three!*"

"MR. LEROY!" the class shouted.

Finally the principal looked up. "I did it!" he said. "I wrote a limerick!"

"It's lunchtime, Mr. Leroy," Gooney Bird said, "and I have a dill-pickle-and-tofu sandwich I am eager to eat."

"May I read my limerick aloud?" the principal asked. The children all nodded. Mrs. Pidgeon looked at the clock again.

Mr. Leroy stood in front of the class. They could see that his paper was covered with eraser marks and cross-outs and scribbles, just like theirs. But he looked very proud.

> A man named John Thomas Leroy
> Hated poetry when just a boy.
>> But the second grade thought
>> That he ought to be taught.
> Soon limericks brought him some joy!

He bowed, and the class applauded politely. "Gotta run," Mr. Leroy said. "I didn't realize it was so late. I have a lunch appointment with the superintendent of schools." Carefully he folded his paper and put it into his pocket. "I think I'll read him my limerick. He might not be familiar with limericks. I wonder if the school board might vote to make limerick writing part of the curriculum."

He said goodbye to the class and disappeared through the door. There was a brief silence. Then Felicia Ann, in her quiet voice, said, "Hith wathn't very good, wath it?"

"Not as good as ours," Barry agreed.

"He just needs more practice," Beanie suggested. "We've been working on poetry for *days*, but it's brand new for him."

"And," Gooney Bird pointed out as she gathered her lunch things, "he probably needs a brain-warming hat."

5.

Mrs. Pidgeon was almost late for school! It had never happened before. Usually she was there early, preparing sharpened pencils, passing out papers, tidying the room.

But on this day she came dashing in at the last minute, her face pink and her eyes teary from the cold. She unwound her long blue scarf and hung it with her coat on the hook.

Then the bell rang. Mrs. Pidgeon scurried to her desk and sat down to catch her breath.

"Very close to tardy, Mrs. Pidgeon!" Gooney Bird said, with a *tsk-tsk* sound.

"I know. I'm sorry. I'm usually here way before you kids."

"Did your toothbrush fall in the toilet?" Malcolm asked. That had happened once to him.

"Did you have a very, very hard time choosing what to wear, and you started to cry because you finally had to wear your red sweater, which you absolutely hated?" asked Chelsea. That had happened once to her.

"Were you stopped by a bus driver asking directions, and it took *forever* to get him to the right place?" Gooney Bird asked. That had happened once to her.

Mrs. Pidgeon shook her head and began to answer, but she was interrupted by the intercom. The class all stood and said the Pledge of Allegiance, led by a sixth-grader named Mary Margaret O'Leary. Then they listened to Mr. Leroy's announcements.

Then, finally, Mrs. Pidgeon explained. "The nursing home called me because my mother had had a bad night. So I went there before I came to school."

"Oh, dear—nightmares?" asked Keiko. "I have nightmares sometimes. My mom gives me warm milk and opens my closet door to show me there aren't monsters."

"Did she wet the bed? Some people wet their beds and it wakes them up," Malcolm said. "Even people as old as eight, sometimes." He looked at the floor.

"Or maybe throw-ups?" asked Ben sympathetically. "I always get the throw-ups in the middle of the night. My mom says if she has to change my sheets one more time at two in the morning . . ."

Mrs. Pidgeon smiled. "No, none of those things. She was just wakeful, and feeling agitated. When they called me, I went and sat with her and we talked. Then she fell asleep so I hurried on to school. I'm sorry, class, but today I didn't remember to bring one of my mother's poems."

"What did you talk about?" Gooney Bird asked. She was at the hamster cage. It was her day to feed Harvey, the class hamster. Harvey had a diet of special pellets, but Gooney Bird felt that he needed something like a buffet to make his life more interesting. So she always arranged his pellets on different paper saucers, and she added bits of lettuce and bread crumbs that she borrowed from people's lunches. Today Harvey was having a smidgen of carrot for his salad course and a fingertip full of raspberry jam for dessert.

"Well, as you know, my mother is very old. So she has a whole lifetime of memories. I asked her to tell me some of the childhood things she remembered as the happiest."

"What did your mom thay?" Felicia Ann asked.

"Let me think." Mrs. Pidgeon half closed her eyes and listed the things her mother had remembered. "Birthday cake with pink candles. A yellow hair ribbon. A kitten named Jingle.

The lace collar on her mother's Sunday dress. Ruffled curtains in her bedroom. A honeysuckle vine. And fireflies."

Gooney Bird closed and latched the door to Harvey's cage. He cleaned the leftover jam from his whiskers carefully and then went to his shredded-paper nest to take a nap. "You know what?" Gooney Bird said to Mrs. Pidgeon. "You *did* bring a poem of your mom's."

"I did?"

"Yes, you just said it. That list of memories. It was just like a poem. If you wrote the memories down on a paper and gave it a title like 'Mom's Memories,' it would even *look* like a poem."

Mrs. Pidgeon thought for a moment and then smiled. "I believe you're right, Gooney Bird. Maybe today at writing time we could each do a list poem. I'll put some ideas for lists here on the board so you can be thinking in advance. But now we'll get out our spelling."

Mrs. Pidgeon wrote four suggestions on the board:

Happy memories
These things make me laugh
Nightmares
Lunches I love

Beside the list, she wrote the day's ten spelling words:

ready
across
thought
brave
threw
because
family
towel
clown
mouse

The children all bent over their desks, copying the words. But they couldn't pay attention to the spelling.

"I'm having a can't-keep-my-thoughts-on-my-work moment," Malcolm announced loudly. "I keep thinking about a list of nightmare stuff."

"Me, too!" Beanie said. "I was trying to write the spelling words, but look!" She held up her paper and everyone could see the eraser marks. "I kept thinking about things that make me laugh!"

"Mrs. Pidgeon, may I make a helpful suggestion?" Gooney Bird had her hand raised. Today she was wearing her diamond ring. It wasn't a real diamond, but it looked like one. It was large and sparkly. Sometimes she let the other girls borrow it. Never boys, though.

"Of course," said the teacher. "What is it?"

"We could combine the spelling words with the list poems. Everybody could try to include some of the spelling words in a poem. That way, we'd kill two birds with one stone."

"Oh, no!" wailed Keiko. "Don't say 'kill birds'!"

"It was just a figure of speech, Keiko," Mrs. Pidgeon reassured her. "It means, ah, well, getting two things done at once. In this case, spelling and poetry writing. I think it's a good idea, Gooney Bird.

"Okay. It can be poetry time, class. List poems today. With some spelling words in them, please."

She passed out fresh pieces of paper. Then she turned her back to the class and went to a section of the board where there was still some blank space. "Here is my mother's poem," she said, and she began to write. She didn't notice that several of the second-graders had opened their desks to take out something.

Mrs. Pidgeon wrote:

It Makes Me Happy to Remember:

A cake with pink candles,
A yellow hair ribbon,
A kitten named Jingle,
The lace collar on my mother's best dress,
Ruffled curtains in my bedroom,

The fragrance of honeysuckle,
And fireflies on summer evenings,
So many fireflies.
I wonder where the fireflies have gone.

When she had finished, she turned to the class. To Mrs. Pidgeon's amazement, seven children—she counted—were now wearing underpants on their heads. Gooney Bird had once again donned her pale green ruffles. Malcolm had tightie-whities, and Ben was wearing boxers with smiley faces. Tricia was wearing white cotton with little blue flowers, and both Beanie and Felicia Ann had pale pink.

"Chelsea?" Mrs. Pidgeon said. "What is that on your head?"

"Thong," Chelsea explained. "Borrowed from my mom."

"And it helps?"

"Oh, yes," all of the children said. "Warms the brain."

"I'm bringin' some tomorrow," Tyrone said. "My brain is *freezin'!*"

"Me, too," said Nicholas.

"Well," Mrs. Pidgeon said with a sigh, "just as long as they are all absolutely clean."

☆ ☆ ☆

As usual, Barry Tuckerman was the first one finished. Now, with his pencil down, his paper neatly folded, his hand shot into the air. "I'm done! I bet mine is the best! I'm the best poet in the class!"

"Poetry is not a contest, Barry," Mrs. Pidgeon reminded him. "There is no best or worst."

"Whatever," Barry said. "Can I read mine?" She nodded, and he stood beside his desk. He read:

These Things Make Me Laugh
by Barry Tuckerman, author

Cartoons
Jokes
My dog
Clowns

Mouse
Towel

Then he sat down.

The class, including Mrs. Pidgeon, was silent for a moment.

Then Gooney Bird gave a loud sigh. "Barry, Barry, Barry," she said. "That was awful."

"You can't say poetry is awful," Barry said. "Poetry is whatever you want it to be."

"But it wath, Barry," Felicia Ann whispered. "It wath thimply awful."

"Did you want it to be unimaginative, Barry? And boring?" Gooney Bird asked.

Barry scowled and shook his head. He looked at his paper. "I guess not," he said finally.

"Well, let's revise," Gooney Bird suggested. "Let's add details. What is funny about these things? Why do they make you laugh?"

Barry shrugged his shoulders. "I don't know."

"Let's take them one at a time. What was your first thing?"

Barry looked at his paper. "Cartoons," he read.

"What makes you laugh about a cartoon?"

"When the superheroes go POW and ZAP," he said.

"Add that, then," Gooney Bird told him. He picked up his pencil. Around the class, other children picked up their pencils again and began to revise their own poems.

"Jokes?" Gooney Bird asked Barry. "Was that next?"

Barry had his tongue between his teeth and was busy writing. "Yeah, I'm adding more about jokes."

"And your dog." Gooney Bird looked around the class. "How many of you have a dog?" Many hands went up. "Do things about your dog make you laugh?"

Everyone nodded. Some children called

out. "My dog's scared of thunder!" Tricia said. "He hides under the bed and we all laugh at him."

Barry looked up. "You know what?" he said. "Clowns don't really make me laugh. I think they're scary."

"Erase 'clowns,' then," Gooney Bird said. "Part of revising is deciding what to take out."

"Barry almost won't have nothin' left in his poem," Tyrone said. He sighed, then corrected himself when he saw Mrs. Pidgeon about to raise her grammar finger. "I mean, Barry won't have anything left. His poem gonna be *short!*"

"Short poems are okay, though," Beanie pointed out.

Barry wasn't listening to anyone. His face was scrunched up again in its thinking position, and he was writing very fast. "Done!" he announced.

"Read it again, Barry," Mrs. Pidgeon said, "and let us hear your revisions."

Barry stood. He read:

Things That Make Me Laugh
by Barry Tuckerman, great author

Cartoons that go
POW
and ZAP!
Jokes, like
Why did the moron?
Or Knock Knock!
And my goofy dog
Because once he chased a mouse
And when my mom threw a towel
Over them
They were both bumps under
     the towel,
The mouse scurrying
And my brave dog ready
to go
POW
And ZAP!

The class laughed and applauded.

"I used six spelling words," Barry said proudly, "and I wrote a good poem."

Gooney Bird went to him and gave him a high-five.

"Ouch," she said. "I should never do that when wearing a diamond ring."

"The really impressive thing," Mrs. Pidgeon said, "is that Barry wrote his list poem without wearing anything on his head except his own hair.

"Maybe hair is enough to warm the brain? What do you think, class?"

But all the second-graders, even those who had not put on brain-warming hats, shook their heads. Even Barry shook his head. "I think I could have done my poem faster and better if my brain had been warmer," he said. "Tomorrow I'm bringing a hat."

Mrs. Pidgeon laughed. "Well," she said, "all right. And maybe tomorrow we can work on a poem for different voices. That's a poem that we recite together, taking different parts."

"Like a play?" asked Beanie.

"A little like a play, I suppose."

"I want a big part," said Chelsea. "I want to be a star!"

"A superstar!" Malcolm said. He stood up and bowed deeply. "Thank you to all my many fans," he said.

6.

A substitute! Mrs. Pidgeon's second grade class had a substitute teacher for the very first time. It was a little scary.

Mr. Leroy entered the classroom with a tall, thin woman and introduced her. "Class," he said, "this is Miss Overgaard. We're fortunate that she was able to substitute at the very last minute. Mrs. Pidgeon has a serious emergency, and she isn't able to come to school today. But she says that she left lesson plans, and I'm sure Miss Overgaard will be able to handle everything just fine.

"You'll let me know if you have any problems?" he said to the tall, thin lady. She wasn't paying any attention to Mr. Leroy. She had carefully taken off her coat, revealing a dark dress with heavy brass buttons, rather like a military uniform, and a pair of glasses dangling from a cord around her neck. Next she reached up to remove the hat she was wearing over her thin straight hair. Ignoring the principal, she hung her coat on the hook behind the door and then placed her hat on the shelf where the dictionaries were stacked. Then, lifting her glasses to sit atop her long nose, she began looking through the drawers of Mrs. Pidgeon's desk.

"Well," he said. "I guess I'll head to my office. This is a fine class," he told Miss Overgaard as he turned to leave the room. "Very creative. Class?" He looked at the children. "See you later—"

"Alligator!" they all responded.

Miss Overgaard jumped. Mr. Leroy smiled at the second-graders, and the door closed behind him.

All of the children, even Gooney Bird Greene, were silent. They watched as the substitute wrote her name on the board in large letters.

MISS OVERGAARD

"Two *a*'s together?" Barry Tuckerman said aloud. "I never saw two *a*'s together before!"

The substitute teacher clapped her hands. "I'll have no calling out!" she said in a firm, loud voice. "Please raise your hand and ask permission if you wish to speak."

The room became silent.

"Good. Now I will read your names from this list, and I expect you to say 'present' when you hear your name called." She began reading from the list, and each child replied.

"Present," said Nicholas nervously.

"Present," Beanie said, looking at the floor.

"Present," Malcolm said loudly, wiggling at his desk.

"Prethent," said Felicia Ann in a whisper.

"Louder, please. More distinctly."

Felicia Ann's face turned pink. "Prethent," she said again.

The substitute teacher looked up from her list. "Repeat that, please."

"Prethent," Felicia Ann repeated miserably.

"Are you receiving speech therapy for your impediment?"

"Excuthe me?" Felicia Ann replied.

"You have a severe lisp. Is the speech therapist seeing you?" the substitute asked.

Felicia Ann looked at the floor.

Gooney Bird's hand shot up. "Permission to speak, Miss Overgaard," she said in a loud voice.

The substitute nodded to her.

Gooney Bird said, "Felicia Ann is missing

her two front teeth. When they grow in, she'll speak just fine. In the meantime, we all think it's rather sweet, the way she talks. And also," Gooney Bird added, "I think it's rude to criticize something that she can't help."

The substitute glared at her. "And you are—?"

"I'm Gooney Bird Greene."

"What kind of ridiculous name is that? And what on earth are you *wearing?*"

Gooney Bird stood beside her desk and looked down at herself. "I'm wearing gray fleece sweatpants from the Gap, and a white ruffled blouse from the Goodwill store—I paid only eighty-nine cents for it and I think it was quite a bargain. I am also wearing bunny slippers, and under the bunny slippers I am wearing one red sock and one yellow sock, because I like a variety of colors; it amuses my feet. And I am wearing a leopard-print vest over my ruffled blouse, and I am wearing a paper Hawaiian lei that my parents brought home from a Polynesian restaurant.

"I am also wearing fake pearl earrings, and in a minute I am going to put on my special brain-warming hat, which is pale green.

"And my name is Gooney Bird, which is a kind of albatross, and my parents named me that because they thought it was unusual and they hoped I would be an unusual person.

"Which I am," Gooney Bird concluded, sitting down. She looked up at Miss Overgaard and added, "Present."

Miss Overgaard glared at her for a moment and then checked off her name in the book.

☆ ☆ ☆

The day did not go well.

First, the substitute announced that she was allergic to all rodents and so the gerbil cage and the hamster cage both had to be removed from the room. Mr. Furillo, the custodian, came to get the cages and promised that he would care for all the class pets in his office; but still, the children could tell that all the gerbils and Harvey, the hamster, were confused and distressed as they were carried out of Mrs. Pidgeon's classroom, the only home they had ever known.

Next, Miss Overgaard looked at Keiko, who was sitting quietly with her hands folded, and asked, "How good is your English?"

Keiko looked up in surprise. "Well, I always get an A in spelling," she said in her soft voice.

"I asked because you appear to be—well, I don't know which, Chinese or Japanese," said the substitute. "I thought you were probably an ESL student. English as a second language."

"Permission to speak," said Gooney Bird again in her firm voice, with her hand raised.

The teacher nodded at her in an irritated way.

Gooney Bird stood, again, beside her desk. "Keiko's American, same as me, and probably you too, Miss Overgaard, even though I bet your parents or grandparents came from some other country, because if you ask me, two *a*'s in a row is very strange—"

"Not in Denmark," Miss Overgaard said with a sniff. "My parents came from Copenhagen."

"Cool. Well, Keiko's grandparents came from Japan. Keiko can even speak Japanese, which is not easy, let me tell you. She tried to teach us some Japanese words for things and I can't remember a single word. Japanese is *hard*."

"Are you finished, miss?" the substitute asked.

"Yes, I am," said Gooney Bird firmly. She sat down. "And don't call me *miss*."

Suddenly Tyrone burst into one of his raps. Sometimes he couldn't help himself. It was the way Tyrone let off steam, Mrs. Pidgeon had once said.

"Day goin' by and people start to cry, 'cuz our teacher be gone and the new one make us yawn—"

"New one make us yawn," the class chanted, repeating part of Tyrone's rap, as they always did. Malcolm got up from his desk and began to dance.

"Rub a dub dub, we doan wanna have a sub—" Tyrone continued.

"Rub a dub dub," chanted the second-graders.

"Silence!" shouted Miss Overgaard. The class obeyed at once.

"Who told you that you could leave your desk?" she said to Malcolm, grabbing his arm. Malcolm began to cry.

"Permission to speak!" said Gooney Bird loudly and then began to speak before Miss Overgaard replied. "Malcolm is hyperactive and dancing is a good way for him to get it out of his system! Mrs. Pidgeon understands that!"

"And she underthtandth my thpeech!" Felicia Ann added.

"And she likes my rap, she doan think I be a sap," chanted Tyrone.

"I want Mrs. Pidgeon back!" Chelsea groaned.

"Me, too!"

"Me, too!"

"We all want Mrs. Pidgeon back!" the class wailed.

Mr. Leroy appeared, suddenly, at the door. "What's the problem here?" he asked. "Mr. Furillo tells me things are not going well in this classroom. Are you giving the substitute teacher a hard time?"

"Make that *former* substitute teacher," Miss Overgaard said. She was putting on her coat. "If you think I'm going to stay one more minute in a classroom that puts up with rodents and rappers and people named for albatrosses . . ."

She stormed out of the room and slammed the door behind her.

The children were wide-eyed at their desks.

"Mr. Leroy," Gooney Bird said, "she was very rude."

"And we didn't even get to do poetry," Beanie added.

"We were going to try poems for different voices today," Tricia explained.

Mr. Leroy looked at his watch. "I think we can manage without an official teacher for a little while. Mr. Furillo and I will be your substitutes today.

"But, class: I have very sad news for you. Mrs. Pidgeon called. Her mother died late this morning."

Keiko gasped, put her head in her arms, and began to cry. All of the children looked shocked and sad.

"Mrs. X!" said Malcolm. "Our room mother!"

"Mrs. Pidgeon wanted all of you to know, before you saw it in tomorrow's paper." Mr.

Leroy went to Keiko's desk and rubbed her head gently while she wept.

"She was very, very old," Chelsea said.

"Yes, everybody dies when they get to be very, very old. My dog died when he was thirteen. That's very, very old for a dog," Ben said with a sigh.

"But thtill it maketh you thad," Felicia Ann pointed out, and Ben nodded.

"Someone bein' dead gives you sadness in your head," Tyrone chanted in a mournful way.

"Mrs. Pidgeon was going to tell us the surprise about her mother's name! But she didn't get a chance to!" Barry Tuckerman reminded them.

"Oh." Mr. Leroy chuckled. "I think I know the surprise. Mrs. Pidgeon had already told me, and I'll tell it to you." He told the class about their room mother's name and spelled it for them.

"Xenia? What kind of name is that?"

Chelsea put her hands on her hips. Mr. Leroy smiled.

"It's Greek," he told the class. "Mrs. Pidgeon's grandparents came from Greece, and her mother had a Greek name. I think the name Xenia actually means 'welcoming.'"

"So when we called her Mrs. X, she really *was* a Mrs. X!" Barry said.

Mr. Leroy nodded. "She thought it was funny, actually. And she was planning to tell you that she really had an *X* name. But then she became ill and she never had the chance."

The children became silent again. It made them sad, thinking about never having the chance.

"Permission to speak?" asked Gooney Bird.

Mr. Leroy smiled. "You don't need to ask formal permission," he said gently. "We always love to hear what you have to say, Gooney Bird."

"I have an idea for something we could do for Mrs. Pidgeon."

"We could make cookies!" Beanie suggested.

"Or thend flowerth," said Felicia Ann.

"This is better than cookies and flowers combined," Gooney Bird said. She began to describe her idea.

7.

"Are you ready, Mr. Leroy?" called Gooney Bird, looking up at the open second-floor window of Watertower Elementary School. She was standing in the snowy school playground with the rest of Mrs. Pidgeon's other second-graders, all of them dressed in boots and jackets and mittens and scarves.

Mr. Leroy was at the window, looking down, and he called back to her, "No, wait!"

"Wait for what? It's cold out here and we're all rehearsed and ready!"

"I'm going to give the camera to Mr. Furillo! I decided I want to be in the video! Is that all right with you?"

"Mr. Leroy, Mr. Leroy, Mr. Leroy," Gooney Bird said with a sigh. "You didn't come to the rehearsal!"

"I know. I was busy in the office because a sixth-grader had a behavior problem in the classroom. I had to have a little talk with him. It wouldn't wait."

"Well, we'll take a vote," Gooney Bird said. "Second-graders? Is it okay if Mr. Leroy is in our video? All in favor say 'Aye'!"

A chorus of ayes came from the playground.

"Any nays?" asked Gooney Bird in a loud voice.

But there was none. The children were silent and smiling.

"Good! Thank you! I'll be right down." Mr. Leroy disappeared from the window, and Mr. Furillo, the custodian, appeared holding the video camera.

Inside the second grade classroom, today's new substitute, a pleasant, chubby man with a beard, was reading while he waited for the class to return. They didn't need him for this project.

"Brrrr," said Mr. Leroy when he arrived on the playground. "Cold out here! Where would you like me?" he asked Gooney Bird.

"Stand near Barry," she directed him, "and do what he does, and say what he says, since you haven't rehearsed. You should have worn your boots, Mr. Leroy," she told him, looking disapprovingly at the snow around his shoes. "Your feet are going to freeze."

"Too late," he said. "I'll just suffer."

He made his way toward Barry and stood beside him.

"All right, everyone!" Gooney Bird shouted. "Listen up! Look toward the camera, and remember your parts! Ready?"

"Ready!" the children called.

"Ready, Mr. Furillo?" called Gooney Bird. "Are you sure you know how to work the camera?"

"Yes," Mr. Furillo replied. "I've done it before!"

"Kids: Remember! Outdoor voices!" Gooney Bird reminded them from where she stood nearest the school building. "Okay, Mr. Furillo! Action!"

She stepped forward, looking up toward the window, where the custodian stood with the camera at his eye. For a second she stood silently. Then, in a booming outdoor voice so that she could be heard on the video, Gooney Bird announced,

"This is a Poem for Many Voices!"

She turned and faced the other children and Mr. Leroy. She held up her arms like a concert director.

"Many Voices!" all of the children called.

Gooney Bird Greene turned back to face the camera. "It is a Goodbye Poem!" she said.

The chorus echoed her. "A Goodbye Poem!"

They all stood silently while Gooney Bird carefully lay down on her back in the snow. She moved her arms up and down, then stood again.

"A snow angel—" she said.

"For Mrs. X!" the children chanted.

Gooney Bird pointed toward Chelsea, who lay down and made another angel, then stood.

"For our room mother!" Chelsea called.

"Our room mother!" the chorus said.

Gooney Bird pointed to Nicholas, who dropped to the ground and made another angel, then stood. "For Xenia!" he called.

"Xenia!" the chorus replied.

As if she were directing a group of instruments, Gooney Bird pointed quickly to Ben, Felicia Ann, and Beanie. They made their angels together and chanted in unison, "And the angels are for her daughter, too!"

The chorus repeated it.

Gooney Bird pointed to Barry. Barry

quickly whispered instructions to Mr. Leroy, and together they lay backwards in the snow and made angels: one small, and one much larger one. "Patricia Pidgeon!" they chanted loudly together, and the chorus repeated the name.

There was a silence, and then Gooney Bird held up both arms and made a gesture. "A good daughter!" everyone chanted.

Another silence. Then: "A good teacher!" they chanted together.

At Gooney Bird's signal, every child—and the principal, following Barry's directions—lay down in the snow. They all moved their arms up and down slowly. From the window where Mr. Furillo was looking down onto the fresh snow that covered the playground, it looked as if a whole flock of birds were preparing to fly.

Then they all stood again, in the outlines of their snow angels.

One by one they each called out a phrase:

Ben: A cake with pink candles!
All: I remember!

Chelsea: A yellow hair ribbon!
All: I remember!

Malcolm: A kitten named Jingle!
All: I remember!

Tricia: The lace collar on my mother's dress!
All: I remember!

Keiko: Ruffled curtains in
my bedroom!
All: I remember!

Felicia Ann: The fragranthe
of honeythuckle!
All: I remember!

Beanie: Fireflies!
Barry and Mr. Leroy: Fireflies!
Tyrone: Fireflies!
All: So many fireflies!

Gooney Bird called, "What happened to all
the fireflies?"

The chorus of children chanted, in reply:

They're out there!
We can't see them!
But Mrs. Pidgeon's mother can!
They're lighting her way!

They all stood silently. Then they held up their hands and waved goodbye.

"This was a Poem for Many Voices," the children said.

After a moment, Mr. Furillo turned the video camera off. They could see him take his rumpled handkerchief from the pocket of his custodian uniform. He wiped his eyes.

The performers left the schoolyard and began to climb the steps to return to school.

"We didn't even wear our poetry hats," Chelsea pointed out.

"It would have been a distraction," Gooney Bird explained, "and anyway, we'd already written the poem. We didn't need to warm our brains for the performance."

"Did you think we did good?" Malcolm asked Mr. Leroy as they entered the school's large front door.

"You did great!" the principal said. He turned and exchanged a high-five with Malcolm. "Just great! I mean, *we* did great. Mrs. Pidgeon will treasure that video, and that poem, forever. It was wonderful.

"We shouldn't boast," he added. Then he looked down at his wet, slush-covered feet, sighed, and said, "My shoes are toast."

Gooney Bird, walking past, had overheard the conversation. She grinned and gave the principal a thumbs-up sign. "Couplet," she said. "Not bad, Mr. L."